NEVER TOO MUCH

Written by
Aundrea Tabbs-Smith

Illustrated by
Vanessa Kaliwo

Books & Things Publishing, LLC.
4410 Brookfield Corporate Dr. #220149 Chantilly, VA 20153

Never Too Much
Text © 2024 Aundrea Tabbs-Smith
Illustrations © 2024 Vanessa Kaliwo
Cover and interior book design by Vanessa Kaliwo

ISBN 978-1-962140-03-4 Hardcover
ISBN 978-1-962140-04-1 Paperback
Library of Congress Control Number 2024902790

For information about bulk purchase or to book an event,
please visit the Books & Things Publishing website,

www.booksandthingspublishing.com

Charlee,

You are a beautiful, funny and intelligent human being.
I love you so much. Keep being you.

You have all the right ingredients.

Charlee loved to bake.

Charlee baked cupcakes

And brownies

And cookies

And cakes

She baked when it rained.

She baked when it snowed.

She baked on cool autumn days.

She baked on humid summer nights.

Charlee baked biscuits

And pies

And cornbread

And muffins

Charlee took her time, measured each ingredient carefully and created delicious sweet treats.

One cool fall day, Charlee was baking with her sous chef, her mom. She was making her famous pumpkin bread. Charlee grabbed a large bowl, a measuring cup and her light blue measuring spoons that her dad bought her for her 6th birthday. In the large bowl she poured in flour, sugar, cinnamon, nutmeg, ginger, baking soda, and salt.

"Oh! I forgot my lucky whisk!" She exclaimed.
Charlee quickly pulled her lucky whisk off it's stand and began mixing the ingredients together. Next, she added, oil, eggs, water, and the most important ingredient, pumpkin purée.
"Can't have pumpkin bread without pumpkin purée!" She said with a chuckle.

Charlee reread the recipe to make sure she added all the right ingredients.

"Oh no! I added *too* much cinnamon! I was only supposed to put in three teaspoons but I put in four! Now I've ruined the pumpkin bread." She said under her breath.

"Hey boo, what's going on in your head right now?" Her mom aka her sous chef asked.

"Well, when I poured in *too* much cinnamon it made me think of something else."

"Really what's that?" Charlee's mom asked.

"Well, people always tell me that I'm too much. They always say I'm being too loud or too dramatic or I'm just too much."

"At school yesterday, Mary said that I was being too loud when I was singing during recess."

"And the day before that Jamal said I was being too dramatic when I said, "Oh my Ganache!" After he spilled his drink at lunch."

"And last week, when I was telling my teacher about our family trip to the aquarium, they told me I was doing too much when I began barking like the seals and moving my body like the jellyfish. I was just excited to share how fun it was."

"Oh, boo. I'm so sorry. How did it make you feel when you were told you were being too loud while you were singing at recess?"
"Well, it made me feel like I shouldn't sing anymore and singing makes me really really happy so that made me feel sad."

"And how did you feel after you were called too dramatic?"
"Well, it made me feel like there was something wrong with how I talked, but I think adding a little extra spice to things makes everything better, so that made me feel upset."

"And what about when you were told you were doing too much when you were sharing about our trip to the acquarium?"
"Well, it made me feel like I shouldn't get excited about things but sharing the fantastic things that happen to me makes me smile on the inside, so that made me feel like..." Charlee thought for a moment...
"It made me feel like being myself was not a good thing."

"Oh, boo. I'm so sorry. I never want you to feel like who you are isn't a good thing. I never want you to feel that you can't be yourself. You have all the right ingredients.

A tablespoon of compassion
A half a cup of creativity
A tablespoon of adventure
A cup of courage
2/3 cups of joy
And a cup of brilliance

All of those ingredients and much, much more, make up who you are. And that, Charlee, will never be too much.

Your beautiful voice
Your acting chops
Your zest for life
Make you an extraordinary human being."

"So repeat after me."
Charlee lifted up her head.

I'm not too much.

I'm not too much.

I'm never too much.

I'm never too much.

Charlee smiled.
"Thanks mom. I feel better.

What are we going to do about the pumpkin bread? I poured in too much cinnamon!"

"Well, a wise person once said, adding a little extra spice to things makes everything better."

And Charlee's mom was right.

That was the best pumpkin bread that Charlee has made
to date.

Charlee's Treats
pumpkin Bread please!
TODAY'S SPECIAL:
PUMPKIN BREAD
$5

Author's Page

Aundrea Tabbs-Smith

is the author of the self-published book, For the Quiet Black Girl: Trying to Find Her Voice in a Predominately White Space.

She has a B.A. in Elementary/Early Childhood Education from Temple University and a Master's in Special Education from Bank Street College of Ed.

She is a former classroom teacher who wants to amplify the voices of Black people through literature.

Printed in the USA
CPSIA information can be obtained
at www.ICGtesting.com
LVHW070846010524
778921LV00001B/1